The Little Book of
Tube Etiquette

By Laura King

Illustrated by Pete Duffield

Gibson Publishing

First published in the UK by Gibson Publishing

The Little Book Of Tube Etiquette
Text copyright 2010 by Laura King
Illustrations copyright 2010 by Pete Duffield

ISBN 978-0-9567101-0-9

Contents

Introduction

I've used the London Underground to commute to work for seven years and have encountered the most weird, wonderful and, at times, frustrating people.

On a rainy evening, having just experienced rush hour in full flow, I went to meet my girlfriends for drinks and quickly we settled into a conversation about all of our irritations about the tube and the people that use it. That turned out to be one of the most hilarious wine-filled catch ups in recent years and provided the inspiration for The Little Book Of Tube Etiquette.

Each 'rule' has a story or experience behind it and the more I've been writing, the more I notice the weird behaviour of our Tube's users. This book isn't meant to be serious, rather a lighthearted attempt to poke fun at the irritations of our daily commute.

I guarantee that once you've read it, you'll never travel to work without noticing the rule-breaks again.

Chapter One

The Unacceptables

Don't get on the tube before others have got off. If you do attempt this, expect a push/shoulder barge/elbow (delete as appropriate) for your troubles. If everyone obeyed this simple mantra, I would be one happy woman.

Don't eat on a tube: that's disgusting – have you no shame? Multiple multiple reasons why not – germs, irritating, messy, smelly… just plain yuck. Even when drunk this is unacceptable. One of my friends ate some greasy fried chicken on the tube on her way home from a drunken night out complete with lip smacking, finger licking noises. A fellow passenger - a stranger - picked up her bag of food and threw it off the tube carriage at the next stop. I applauded.

Wash. Do you have any idea how unpleasant rush hour is at the best of times without my nose against your unwashed armpit?

Loud music.

I DON'T want to hear your music, especially not over mine *and* when you are on one side of the carriage and I'm on the other. Those dirty looks ARE aimed at you and deservedly so. Cross reference: personal space, and 'how to get your own back at perennial rule breakers.'

Mobile phones.

I DON'T want to hear your conversation and I DON'T want to hear your ridiculous 1970s TV show style ringtone. You are not cool, popular or trendy. Just an irritant.

Never discuss the end of books, movies or tv shows that you have seen. One simply evil woman ruined the ending of Harry Potter's final book for me just two days after it was released – give me a flippin chance!

Cover your mouth when you cough – I don't

want your germs and I'm sure you don't want to be the reason for the 21st century spread of the plague. I caught swine flu thanks to someone sneezing on my face - yes, I felt it too.

In fact, if you are ill, don't use the tube at all.

Stilettos.

If you have to wear them on the tube, please please PLEASE watch where you are standing. I have actually had a broken toe due to a stiletto on a tube and the culprit still looked at me like it was my fault for being in the way.

When carrying bags or shopping, put these on the floor. The continuous banging into my leg isn't just annoying – it HURTS and is tantamount to actual bodily harm.

Chapter Two

The Just-commonsensicals

Personal space. Don't read my paper over my shoulder. Just because I happen to stand or sit next to you does NOT give you special permission to invade my personal space, whether you are genuinely reading my paper or just thinking I haven't noticed you looking down my top whilst disguised as reading my paper. YOU KNOW WHO YOU ARE.

Don't talk to strangers. Londoners are rude – just deal with it.
The tube is not a place of socialising. A smile is the limit.

Drunken flirting. Just because you are bladdered, it doesn't mean that you can try it on with the girl sitting opposite to you. And, realistically, you are more likely to frighten them by your slurring and inappropriateness. The 'no talking rule' still applies 24 hours a day, 7 days a week.

Please don't carry **hot coffee** on the tube. I don't trust you not to spill it all over me. Actually change that to don't carry any coffee on the tube. Even if I'm not scalded, I will still breathe fire if you stain my clothes.

Travelling with small children or babies in rush hour – you are simply cruel. To our ears, and your children's nightmares.

Don't run/fight for a seat. This is simply sad and the standing will do you good. Pushing someone out of the way for a seat is desperate, pathetic and worthy of people laughing at you. That's right; AT you - not with you.

Don't lean on the doors of the carriage.

The announcer is talking to YOU Mr leaner. (See learn English as a cross reference). YOU are the reason I am late for work and YOU are the reason the tube keeps stopping and breaking. You have no right to grumble about the tube's slowness – it is your fault.

Don't hold the door open if it is closing. If the door is closing, you missed your train – wait for the next one. Don't break the tube for the rest of us. Once, someone shoved their arm in the tube door and was dragged along the platform – karma.

If you are **massively overweight,** please don't sit down – the standing will do you good. You are effectively taking up two seats (and in some cases I've witnessed – three seats). This is, of course, unfair unless you have bought two tickets and thus paid twice as much as the rest of us. It is as bad as putting your bags on the seat next to you.

Don't put your bags on the seat next to you. No matter how empty the tube is when you get on it you WILL have to move your bags and DON'T give me the evil eye when I want to sit down on the seat where your bags are. I've paid my ticket and I'm sure your bags haven't. Again, unless you've paid for two tickets, you only get one seat (and, let's face it, sometimes no seat).

Chapter Three

Essential etiquette

If you live outside of zone two and actually get a **signal,** don't try and use your mobile phone when reception is dodgy. Shouting 'hello' repeatedly is torture to our ears.

Don't sing on the tube – you are not auditioning for a talent show, and will not be 'spotted'. There is one special circumstance when this is allowed – see 'how to get your own back'.

Don't laugh out loud when reading a paper, book or text message, it's not funny enough to warrant a laugh-out-loud moment, trust me oh attention seeker.

We all understand as a rule of engagement that the tube is not always reliable, on time or without fault. However, the continuous cursing, heavy breathing or shaking of one's head is just not on. Don't project your obvious anger management issues on innocent fellow passengers who feel the same but are able to keep their annoyance well-contained.

Continuous **ruffling** through your **bag** is not on.

I don't like being elbowed at the best of times, but not for the entire 40 minutes of my journey to work, fidget. Crossword enthusiasts – this also applies to you. Oh, and for that measure, teachers – if you are marking work on the tube on the way in, you clearly haven't done your homework. It's not our fault and thus don't do it and bruise us in the meantime. And for all of those who apply make-up on the tube, get up five minutes earlier - it will be kinder to our eyes and ribs.

If you are in the way of the tube door, get off and let the people behind you off. The tube won't go without you and, if it does, it is probably karma for a previous tube offence.

Sex pests – I know it is jammed, but do you need to linger your hand against my bottom?

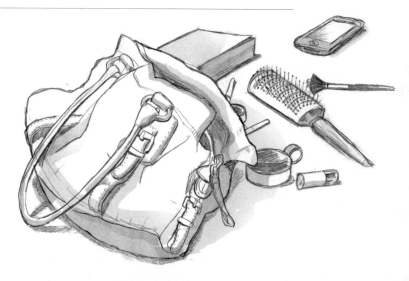

Don't hurl yourself onto the tube when it is packed. **Ouch.**
Is it really worth potentially wounding someone to get to work one minute earlier? You may expect a push back off if this type of behaviour continues.

Tourists – why travel to London in rush hour? It is, quite simply, selfish. And a further strain on the tube network itself. Why would you want to put yourself through that anyway?

Learn English... you are in England, no? This will enable you to understand what the announcer is saying and will probably mean you no longer talk over the announcement that I am so desperately trying to hear myself.

If you are speaking in a foreign language but still looking at us, it is no longer a secret that you are talking about us. Also, some of us speak other languages too. N'est-ce pas?

PDAs – public displays of affection. What, pray tell, is romantic about our stinking underground travel system? The slurping noises are not on, and in some cases I have been sprayed by over-affectionate snogging - please no.

Arguing. Have you no dignity? Save your troubles for the confines of your own house.

Shrieking – why is shouting necessary on a tube? We don't all want to hear you no matter how excited or attention-seeking you are.

If you must play computer games, turn the sound OFF.

Umbrellas are weapons – use them wisely. Also, don't shake your umbrella off when it's been raining, or balance it against my leg. Thanks.

Men – if you have had one of the following the night before then extensive mouthwash, tooth brushing and consumption of mints is required BEFORE you get on the tube: curry, garlic or more than three pints of beer. If you have had more than nine pints, we can also smell the alcohol coming from your sweat pores - consider two showers.

DON'T use the tube if you have a tendency to be sick with a hangover. Fainting, vomiting or anything that makes us have to pull the emergency stop lever is frankly the most selfish thing you can do. We become late; have to give up our seat, and smell of sick.

Always have tissues on your personage. Perennial sniffers are the pits. And, don't think we don't notice you reverting to a primary schooler and wiping your nose on the sleeve of your shirt or worse, on your hand, then wiping your hand on the seat. EUGGGGHHHHHH.

If you are standing up, it is only polite to sit down if the seat directly in front or behind you is vacated. Movement towards any other seat is simply stealing from someone else.

Pregnant women – please wear a sticker so that we know, for sure, you are pregnant and genuinely deserve a seat. It will also stop us from potentially upsetting the more rotund.

Don't carry on trying to have a conversation with your friend when: they are sitting opposite to you or more than one seat away from you and there are people in between. And don't, and I've been on the receiving end of this myself, physically move someone out of the way so you can carry on your conversation. You know who you are, little miss central line.

Don't fall asleep on my shoulder. This is not funny but rather a gross invasion of my personal space. We are strangers and this is just not acceptable.

Chapter Four

Station etiquette

Have your **Oyster cards** ready! This enables the flow of the cattle herd tramplers to continue without stopping, prevents the backlog of queues in the station and minimises irritable commuters swearing under their breath (although to be fair you will always see some of these!). This particularly applies to Oxford Circus and Victoria stations that often have to shut the station concourse due to excessive queuing at the barriers.

Don't stand in the way of the platform entrance or exit. What is the matter with you? You have no right to be upset if people get irritated and 'accidentally' bump you on the way past as you block the hundreds of passengers trying to get on to the platform.

Don't get to the front of the queue at the ticket office and THEN decide to plan your journey. This is simply bad taste and presumably only done to annoy others queuing, otherwise there's just no reason for it other than sheer stupidity.

Don't stop after you've gone through the ticket barriers. In case you don't know how the tube stations work, imagine a steady stream of traffic. People won't stop and walk around you, they are officially in 'Commuter' mode. Definition of 'Commuter mode': a robot-like android state of consciousness with little regard for dawdlers, moving as part of a cattle herd and likely to trample.

Be aware that the clocks on the platforms are slow. When they say 2 minutes, they really mean 4 minutes, believe me – when I'm bored I count the seconds to test them and almost all are 2 seconds to every real second. So, with this fact now in mind, there is no need to stamp your feet/kick the ground /swear profusely/or utter the lines 'longest three minutes I've ever seen' whilst waiting.

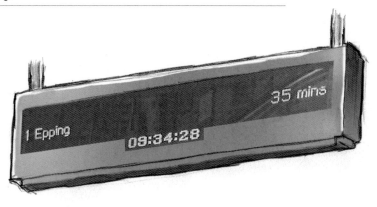

If the platform is busy and **people are queuing** for the tube, cleverly lined up where the carriage doors are likely to stop don't just join this queue, the chances are, that one person stopped there in the beginning as a guess and others merely thought they knew something others didn't. Take a chance – stop somewhere else and watch as they all look annoyed when you manage to get on board or, even better, get a seat! And for the rest of us walking along the platform, at least we'll be able to get past the queues if you're all spread out more. Double whammy!

If you can hear the tube doors closing as you are coming down the stairs towards the platform, don't start pushing past people and sprinting along the platform. Odds on, you WILL injure someone and still miss the damn tube. The great thing about the tube is there will hopefully be another one along in about 2 minutes so be patient, polite and less of a bruiser to humankind.

There is a reason why there are signs saying 'keep to the right' on escalators - so that those who are, God forbid, in a hurry or like to actually exercise can walk up ahead of the people not moving. There is nothing worse than someone sprawling any which way over the escalator and causing a bottleneck of increasingly angry human traffic behind. This also applies to shopping bags, public displays of affection and those in their own little worlds. This is not the time or place.

While gentle hurrying is of course permitted, full-out running for a train is most definitely not. I've been knocked over by someone hurtling for the nearest carriage door without a moment's thought to my welfare. Imagine if you'd just knocked down an elderly lady? You are going to be late for your appointment, accept that and leave earlier next time to save adding ABH to your list of crimes.

Chapter Five

How to get a seat

If single, **smile sweetly** at a young man who is seated. With any luck he'll sense the opportunity to impress and jump up quicker than you can say 'nice suit'.

If you have a **boyfriend,** position him a little further up the area between the seats so he can save you the seat if the one directly in front or behind him becomes vacant. Others may hate you for it but it's a perfectly acceptable method. If he takes the seat instead, dump him!

Carry big or multiple bags. These can be empty but noone else needs to know that. Couple it with some looks of anguish and swapping your arms over to hold them will add to the act. Someone is bound to give you a seat if they think you are struggling.

When you get on the tube, aim to get right **in the middle** of the two rows of seats. Even if the train is packed, some purposeful and continuous, but not aggressive, edging towards this area is advised.

If you are standing in between the two rows of seats the unspoken rule is that the seat directly in front and behind you is yours. If someone gets up from one of these two areas, you are entitled to that seat and if anyone else moves towards it, hold your space.

Be prepared. As the tube moves towards the next station, tell-tale signs of people likely to disembark are: the closing of books, the squinting at the tube map to see what the next station is, looking out of the window or any other sort of fidgeting which looks like they are preparing for something. This preparation will give you the edge over other seat hopefuls.

If an **elderly** person or **pregnant** woman is standing next to you and noone is letting them sit down, shame them. Try looking at the person who is least likely to give up their seat and say 'excuse me, do you think you could give up your seat for this person', they will be so embarrassed you will have shamed them into jumping up like a jack-in-the-box. Then, if you're really lucky someone else sitting next to them will also jump up and then instead of sitting back down again may offer you their seat instead. Sketchy and not always successful but at least you look like a saint for standing up for other commuters.

If all else fails and you are still desperate for a seat and need to step things up a bit try feeling your forehead, shifting on your feet and fanning yourself. People will be scared you'll faint and decide that delaying their journey trumps having a comfortable journey so may offer you theirs.

Chapter Six

Rules if I were Mayor

Yellow cards and red cards will be distributed by hidden 'tube detectives' for repeat offenders for any of the below rules.

Mobile phones will be **confiscated** if seen to be used in any cases that are not emergencies. For all other reasons, a text will suffice as long as the sound is firmly switched off. Your mobile will be returned to you after your journey along with, if deemed appropriate, a yellow card as a warning.

Everyone who is standing MUST hold on to the handrail. If you don't you will harm, injure and possibly maim.

Tourists and parents with **young children** are only allowed on the tube between 10am and 4pm then 7pm until closing.

All ladies must carry their high heels in a separate bag to change into at work and, while travelling on the tube, must wear flats at all times.

If anyone can hear your music so that they can identify the song or any of the words, it is too loud and any one of those people are hereby sanctioned to remove the offending article.

Two tickets must be purchased for all men over 18 stone and all women size 20 and over. Sorry – this isn't fattist, it's practical.

If the tube breaks down or you are stuck in a tunnel for 10 minutes or longer, all those with a seat should swap with their nearest standers.

No food or drink allowed on tube – apart from a bottle of water that is small enough to fit in a handbag. That's all folks.

If you are deemed too ill to travel on the tube, you will be banned for two whole days until you can prove health.

Chapter Seven

How to get your own back at perennial rule breakers

If someone keeps reading your **newspaper** over your shoulder, point the page in their direction as if you are making it easier for them to see. They'll be so embarrassed they won't do it again.

Another deterrent to over the shoulder paper readers is, if you have almost finished your paper anyway, fold it up and leave it on your lap.

Always carry tissues with you, if someone is sniffing offer them one. It will shame them so much that they will never forget tissues again.

If someone's phone keeps going off, pretend to answer yours but say in an overly loud whisper in the mouthpiece 'hi, sorry I didn't answer straight away, my phone is on silent. Can I call you back, I'm on the tube and I don't want to annoy the other passengers.

If someone is **shrieking** or shouting on the tube, cover your ears or rub your temples as if you have a headache – they'll soon get the message.

If someone has their music on loud, sing along – they'll soon turn it down.

If the person sitting next to you is a fidget or, better still, constantly searching through their bag, say 'let me give you some more room until you find what you are looking for' or something similar. Again, they are likely to find said item immediately!

If someone is eating on the tube, hold your nose! Or, if someone is sitting next to you eating, keep brushing off imaginary (or if it's bad, real) crumbs. Perhaps they'll think twice.

If someone is wearing **high heels** and treads on your foot, grimace and rub your foot repeatedly. Hopefully the offender will feel so bad they'll wear flats next time. Or, if they are falling about all over the place – I'm thinking Central Line's interesting ability to weave and jump about on the tracks – act as if you are being friendly and joke to them 'bet you wish you'd worn flats now', your point will be made in the disguise of a friendly comment.

If someone is on the phone and being loud, get the eye contact of as many people sitting around them and roll your eyes. I guarantee at least half of them will respond in the same way and smile – the offender is bound to notice this and you wont look like the only one annoyed - power and safety in numbers!

Chapter Eight

Funniest announcements heard on the tube

"I'm sorry that you are experiencing delays to your journey, but we are experiencing the wrong sort of rain…" Which begs the question - what sort of rain is the 'wrong sort'? The tube is mostly an UNDERGROUND train, it shouldn't be affected by any kind of rain.

"There are delays because…well, it's the Central Line innit"
well – quite.

"Can people please not lean on the doors of the tube. Can people PLEASE not lean on the doors… oh for goodness sakes, lady in pink with the beret, what's that about? I'm talking to you. MOVE." Love it when they name and shame.

"There are delays to your journey because of communication problems" What? Does this mean you don't TALK to each other and that's the problem?

"You are at Shepherds Bush, next stop White City." (Repeated in five different languages) Oh alright, show off. What are you doing as a tube driver if you can speak FIVE languages??

"Right, to whoever is holding the doors open, everyone wants to go to work. I don't care, I'm at work." Genius.

"We will be waiting at this station because someone has soiled one of the carriages. We are currently waiting for someone to clear up this soilage. We will not be calling for emergency help as this is not an emergency – unless someone decides to make it one by getting their own back on the soiler." Eh?

"May I remind everyone that as of last week, it is now illegal to consume alcohol on the tube. However, if someone was to drop off a bottle of vodka for the driver, I suppose I could turn a blind eye." Drink driving anyone?

Acknowledgements

Firstly I would like to thank my wonderful friends: Ginny, Paula, Dave and Kate, who all provided input on that memorable wine-soaked evening and in turn inspired the book to come about. The wine is on me next time guys.

Secondly, my thanks must go to my husband-to-be who kept the pressure on me to finish and perfect the book, even when I was sick of travelling on the tube, never mind writing about it.

Thirdly, thank you to Pete Duffield, an amazingly talented artist who illustrated the book perfectly, bringing all the wonderful characters to life.

Finally, my thanks must go to all of the people who use the tube that inspired the characters - please don't take any offence, as I said it really is a lighthearted attempt to poke fun - without which, I wouldn't have had so much entertainment recounting the many stories with my friends, and I certainly would never have been able to write this book without you.

Laura.